# Landscape
## Inspirations

A Collection of Drawing and Painting Ideas for Artists

Includes work in:
- Acrylic
- Oil
- Pastel
- Watercolor

First published in the United States of America by:
Quarry Books, an imprint of
Rockport Publishers, Inc.
33 Commercial Street
Gloucester, Massachusetts 01930-5089
Telephone: (508) 282-9590
Fax: (508) 283-2742

Distributed to the book trade and art trade in the United States by:
North Light Books, an imprint of
F & W Publications
1507 Dana Avenue
Cincinnati, Ohio 45207
Telephone: (800) 289-0963


Other Distribution by:
Rockport Publishers
Gloucester, Massachusetts 01930-5089

ISBN 1-56496-384-5

10 9 8 7 6 5 4 3 2 1

Designer: **Frederick Schneider / Grafis**
Cover Images: Front cover, left to right: pp. 68, 16, 102
background: p. 120
Back cover, left to right: pp. 127, 46, 100

Printed in Hong Kong.

# *Landscape* Inspirations

A Collection of Drawing and Painting Ideas for Artists

ROCKPORT PUBLISHERS, INC. • GLOUCESTER, MASSACHUSETTS

DISTRIBUTED BY NORTH LIGHT BOOKS • CINCINATTI, OHIO

# Introduction

A landscape is defined as a portion of land or territory that the eye can comprehend in a single view. This may be a book of landscapes, but what you will find in this volume is much more than that: each of these paintings will give you the opportunity to see a landscape through eyes of another person.

Every person perceives the world around them in a very different way. This happens for a number of reasons, both mental and physical. Previous experiences and personal background will have an affect, just as the amount of rods and cones in your eyes changes color and depth perception. Each of these paintings captures not so much the actual landscape as the way the painter sees the landscape. Whether the painting has true-to-life details or abstract forms, each of these paintings gives you the chance to look at a scene through someone else's eyes. And what variety that produces! From the abstract forms of one painting to the carefully detailed blades of grass on another, each of these paintings exudes style and talent.

But the artists' views are not the only thing you will find in these paintings. Consider the many different levels at which paintings can be examined: content, technique, style, application. First, of course, is the examination of the choice of site, whether it be the country, the city, or even a boatyard, there is an incredible amount to see and paint. Secondly, there is the painter's technique. Every painter has so many choices at the start of a painting: whether to paint en plein air or in a studio; what paper to use; what brushes to use; what media to use. Every detail will have an impact on the finished product. And of course, the examination of the style of painting, whether abstract or realistic, it is almost fun to notice and realize the influence of other artists and styles on a painting.

A landscape may be able to be comprehended by the eye in a single view, but these paintings offer so many more levels of comprehension. No single viewing will be enough. The amount of inspiration you will find, in subject, style, and technique, is extensive. We hope that you will enjoy this collection and take the time to see it on every possible level.

**Dorothy Sandlin**
*Dunes in October*
18" × 24" (45.7 cm × 61 cm)
*Sennelier La Carte pastel paper*

**Joyce Nagel**
*Dune Path*
21.5" × 27.5" (54.6 cm × 69.9 cm)
*Pastel with turpentine*
*Ersta fine grit sandboard*

**Wilma Wethington**
*Falls Mill*
29" x 40" (73.7 cm x 101.6 cm)
*Canvas*

**Jeffrey L. Barnhart**
*Memorial Square-Chambersburg, PA*
36" x 48" (91.4 cm x 121.9 cm)
*Stretched canvas*

**Jack Jones**
*Trinity Church*
21" x 29"  (53.3 cm x 73.7 cm)
*Arches 140 lb. cold press*

**Don O'Neill, A.W.S.**
*Old Fox Theater*
20" x  28"  (50.8 cm x 71.1 cm)
*Bockingford 140 lb. cold press*

**Harvey Dinnerstein**
*Morning Light, Brooklyn*
17.75" x 22.5" (45.1 cm x 57.2 cm)
*Board*

**Lawrence Wallin**
*Hidden Valley*
36" × 48" (91 cm × 122 cm)
*Canvas*

**Fred MacNeill**
*From the Bridge*
16" x 12" (40.6 cm x 30.5 cm)
*Board*

**Jann T. Bass**
*High Fall*
12" x 8" (30.5 cm x 20.3 cm)
*Gesso-primed composition board*

**Fred L. Messersmith,
A.W.S., W.H.S.**
*Maine Moods*
22" × 30"  (55.9 cm × 76.2 cm)
*Arches 300 lb. cold press*
*Media: Watercolor, gouache*

**William Welch**
*Summer Solace*
14" × 21" (35.6 cm × 53.3 cm)
*Linen*

**Petr Liska**
*Bohemian Highlands*
24" x 30" (61 cm x 76 cm)
*Canvas*

**Lynn Tornberg**
*Irish Green*
37" x 37" (94 cm x 94 cm)
*Canvas*

**Judy Pelt**
*Sundance*
22" x 28" (55.9 cm x 71.1 cm)
*Sanded pastel paper*

**Connie Kuhnle**
*Vessels*
24" x 19" (61 cm x 48.3 cm)
*Canson Mi-Teintes paper*

**Gerald F. Brommer**
*Cuenca Facade*
48" × 36" (122 cm × 91 cm)
Acrylic with washi (rice paper)
Canvas

**Christopher Leeper**
*Volant*
22" x 30" (56 cm x 76 cm)
*Arches 140 lb. cold press watercolor paper*

**Philip Jamison**
*Horseshoe Hills*
9.5" x 14.5"  (24.1 cm x 36.8 cm)
*Cold press*
*Media:  Watercolor, charcoal*

**Clark G. Mitchell**
*Autumn Grapevines*
15" x 21.5" (38.1 cm x 54.6 cm)
*Pastel with turpentine*
*La Carte pastel paper*

**Diana Randolph**
*Rocky Mountain Wildflowers*
18" x 24" (45.7 cm x 61 cm)
*La Carte 200 lb. pastel card*

**Kevin M. Donahue**
*Sonoma Memory*
12" × 18" (30.5 cm × 45.7 cm)
*Oil-primed linen canvas*

**Kathy Shumway-Tunney**
*Morning-Hill Top Park © 1995*
19" × 25" (48.3 cm × 63.5 cm)
*German fine-grit sanded pastel paper*

**Paul Strisik, N.A., A.W.S.**
*Hyde Park, London*
14" x 21" (35.6 cm x 53.3 cm)
*J.B. Green 300 lb. cold press*

**Joan Boryta**
*Hallowed Ground*
15" x 22" (38.1 cm x 55.9 cm)
*Winsor & Newton 140 lb. cold press*

**Steven L. Babecki**
*Last Flight*
27" × 37" (69 cm × 94 cm)
*Strathmore #112 cold press
watercolor board*

**Steven L. Babecki**
*Ocala Country*
29" × 39" (74 cm × 99 cm)
*Strathmore #112 cold press watercolor board*

**Bonnie Fergus**
*Harbor Sail*
18" x 24" (46 cm x 61 cm)
*Prestretched canvas*

**Linda Kessler**
*San Miguel de Allende, México*
12" x 28" (30 cm x 71 cm)
*Canvas*

**Anatoly Dverin**
*My Backyard*
12" x 16" (30.5 cm x 40.6 cm)
*Canson Ingres pastel paper, tint #55*

**Carol Lopatin**
*Shenandoah Valley*
29" × 41" (74 cm × 104 cm)
*Arches 555 lb. cold press watercolor paper*

**Carol Lopatin**
*Davis Mountains High Pastures*
29" × 41" (74 cm × 104 cm)
*Arches 555 lb. cold press watercolor paper*

**Joe Jaqua**
*Powell Street, San Francisco*
18" x 25"  (45.7 cm x 63.5 cm)
*300 lb. cold press*

**Marge Chavooshian**
*Harbor in Portovenera*
22" x 30"  (55.9 cm x 76.2 cm)
*Arches 140 lb. cold press*

**Joyce Garner**
*Source (Orpheus and Eurydice Series)*
66" x 60" (167.6 cm x 152.4 cm)
*Linen Canvas*

**Barbara Goodspeed**
*Near the Brook*
20" x 24" (50.8 cm x 61 cm)
Canvas

**Carol Lopatin**
*Davis Mountains Voladera*
29" x 41" (74 cm x 104 cm)
*Arches 555 lb. cold press*
*watercolor paper*

**Monroe Leung**
*Pawn Shop*
15.5" × 22" (38.4 cm × 55.9 cm)
*Arches 140 lb. cold press*

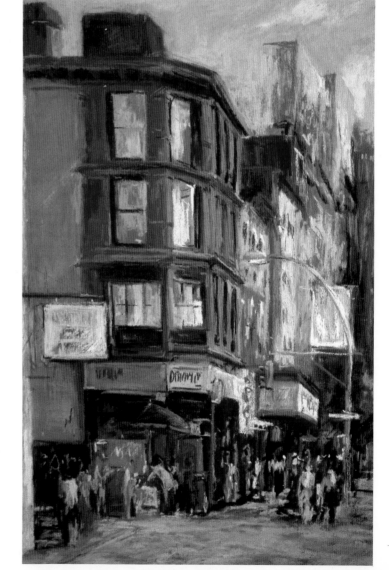

**Lorrie B. Turner**
*Going About Business*
28" × 20" (71.1 cm × 50.8 cm)
*Pastel with gesso and acrylic Gesso-, pumice-
and acrylic-textured 100% rag acid-free
hand-made museum board*

**Donna Levinstone**
*Season Suite IV*
15" x 19" (38.1 cm x 48.3 cm)
*Stonehenge paper*

**Donna Levinstone**
*Season Suite I*
15" x 19" (38.1 cm x 48.3 cm)
*Stonehenge paper*

**Giovanni Martino**
*Morning Clouds*
42" × 60" (106.7 cm × 152.4 cm)
*Linen canvas*

**Coralie Alan Tweed**
*Roan Mt. Blackberry Bushes*
25" × 32" (63.5 cm × 81.3 cm)
*Pastel with gouache and gesso*
*Arches 130 lb. hot press paper*

**Elizabeth M. Mowry**
*September*
20" × 38" (50.8 cm × 96.5 cm)
*Sanded board*

**Coralie Alan Tweed**
*The Sentinels*
40" × 51" (101.6 cm × 129.5 cm)
*Pastel with gouache and gesso*
*Gesso-coated Strathmore*
*400 paper*

**Desmond O'Hagan**
*American Bar, Paris*
16.5" x 22" (41.9 cm x 55.9 cm)
*Canson Mi-Teintes paper*

**Desmond O'Hagan**
*Dinner at Eight, Paris*
18.5" x 25.5" (47 cm x 64.8 cm)
*Canson Mi-Teintes paper*

**Susan Lucas Updyke**
*Spirit of the Sierra*
40" × 60" (102 cm × 152 cm)
Canvas

**Judith Surowiec**
*When the Fog Rolls In*
22" × 23" (56 cm × 58 cm)
Linen canvas

**Mark Flickinger**
*Highland Stream*
36" x 48" (91.4 cm x 121.9 cm)
*Canvas*

**Violet Baxter**
*Nocturne*
22.5" × 31" (57.2 cm × 78.1 cm)
*Canterbury handmade 170 lb. cover paper*

**Anne Heywood**
*Side Street*
20" × 30" (50.8 cm × 76.2 cm)
*Granular board*

**Everett Raymond
Kinstler, N.A., A.W.S., P.S.A.**
*Waterfront, London*
6" × 10" (15.2 cm × 25.4 cm)
*Slightexture P & O hot press*

**Bruce G. Johnson**
*Hurryin' Harvest*
21" × 29" (53.3 cm × 73.6 cm)
*Arches 300 lb. cold press*

**Sandra Humphries**
*Good Morning, Albuquerque*
22" × 30"  (55.9 cm × 76.2 cm)
*Arches 300 lb. cold press*
*Media:  Transparent watercolor, acrylic*

**Gloria Paterson**
*Lite Plane Space I*
22" × 31"  (55.9 cm × 78.7 cm)
*Rives BFK, primed with gesso*

**Kristi Krafft**
*Late Afternoon Glow Through the Oaks*
16" x 30" (40.6 cm x 76.2 cm)
*Linen*

**Murray Muldofsky**
*Mississippi Landscape*
10" x 18" (25.4 cm x 20.3 cm)
*Canvas mounted on panel*

**Lois Salmon Toole**
*Park Avenue Perspective*
27.75" x 20.5"  (70.2 cm x 51.8 cm)
*Arches 300 lb. cold press*

**Becky Haletky**
*Sun Shower*
20" x 28"  (50.8 cm x 71.1 cm)
*Arches 140 lb. rough*

**Judith Surowiec**
*Peekskill Crossing*
20" x 24" (51 cm x 61 cm)
*Linen canvas*

**Judith Surowiec**
*Summer House*
32" x 21" (81 cm x 53 cm)
*Linen canvas*

**Coralie Alan Tweed**
*Autumn Brilliance*
48" × 60" (121.9 cm × 152.4 cm)
*Pastel with gouache and gesso*
*Gesso-coated Strathmore 400 paper*

**Donald L. Berry**
*Red Hots*
20" × 23" (50.8 cm × 58.4 cm)
*Masonite*

**Babette Martino**
*Study for:  Blue Moon over Three Mile Island*
11.75" x 20" (29.9 cm x 50.8 cm)
*Masonite panel*

**Martin R. Ahearn, A.W.S.**
*Moonlite, Rockport Harbor*
45" × 30" (114.3 cm × 76.2 cm)
*Arches Elephant 240 lb.*

**Margaret M. Martin**
*Salute to Soldiers and Sailors*
22" × 30" (55.9 cm × 76.2 cm)
*Arches 300 lb. cold press*

**Richard Brzozowski**
*Meat Market*
30" x 40" (76 cm x 102 cm)
*Bainbridge #181 cold press
watercolor board*

**Richard Brzozowski**
*City Lights*
29" x 40" (74 cm x 102 cm)
*Bainbridge #181 cold press
watercolor board*

**Lorrie B. Turner**
*Land's End*
18" x 24" (45.7 cm x 61 cm)
*Canson Mi-Teintes paper*

**Carole Chisholm Garvey**
*Shadows on the Beach*
10" x 15" (25.4 cm x 38.1 cm)
*Canson paper*

**Dong Kingman**
*Red Sail & East Wind*
22" x 30"  (55.9 cm x 76.2 cm)
*Arches 300 lb.*

**Judith S. Rein, M.W.S.**
*From the Damascus Gate*
18" x 24"  (45.7 cm x 60.9 cm)
*Stonehenge cream printing paper*

**Lynne Lockhart**
*Dead Battery*
22" × 16" (55.9 cm × 40.6 cm)
*Canvas duck*

**Carole Chisholm Garvey**
*Sampson's Island, Fall*
11.5" × 10" (29.2 cm × 25.4 cm)
*Canson paper*

**Gerri Brutschy**
*Reflections*
28" × 22" (71.1 cm × 55.9 cm)
*Stretched canvas*

**Glenn Moreton**
*Venice: Vans*
24" × 46" (61 cm × 117 cm)
*Canvas*

**Glenn Moreton**
*Chinatown Shul*
26" x 48" (66 cm x 122 cm)
*Canvas*

**Glenn Moreton**
*Rodeo*
24" x 36" (61 cm x 91 cm)
*Canvas*

**Frank P. Corso**
*The Road to Sankaty*
24" x 36" (61 cm x 91.4 cm)
*Canvas fixed to board*

**Frank P. Corso**
*Late Light in Monomoy*
24" x 30" (61 cm x 76.2 cm)
*Canvas fixed to board*

## Murray Wentworth, N.A., A.W.S.
*Wintered Ridge*
23" x 33" (58.4 cm x 83.8 cm)
*Strathmore medium surface*

### Howard Huizing
*Mist Trail*
36" x 18" (91.5 cm x 71.1 cm)
*Arches 140 lb. cold press*

### Benjamin Mau, N.W.S.
*Hedge Apples*
24" x 30" (60.9 cm x 76.2 cm)
*Arches 140 lb. cold press*

**Gaye Elise Beda**
*Venetian Triptych*
25" x 42"
(64 cm x 107 cm)
*Portrait linen*

**Glenn Moreton**
*Castro Gas*
26" x 48" (66 cm x 122 cm)
*Canvas*

**Barry G. Pitts**
*Autumn Contrast*
23" × 27.5" (58.4 cm × 69.9 cm)
*Pastel with turpentine*
*Sanded board*

**Phyllis J. Friel**
*Window Rock*
19" × 25" (48.3 cm × 63.5 cm)
*007 Sanded paper*

**Frank P. Corso**
*Moonrise Over Gloucester*
24" x 30" (61 cm x 76.2 cm)
*Canvas fixed to board*

**Merriel Taylor**
*The Water Dance*
11" x 18" (27.9 cm x 45.7 cm)
*Ersta 7/0 sandpaper*

**Cheryl O'Halloran-McLeod**
*Las Primeras Nieves del Ontono*
21" x 24" (53.3 cm x 61 cm)
*Sanded board*

**Lynn Tornberg**
*Our Lady*
26" x 38" (66 cm x 97 cm)
*Canvas*

**Lynn Tornberg**
*Hampden Hill*
31" x 25" (79 cm x 64 cm)
*Canvas*

**Ward P. Mann**
*Cape Pond Ice House*
24.5" x 32.5" (62.2 cm x 82.6 cm)
*Panel*

**Ward P. Mann**
*Rocky Neck*
22" x 28" (55.9 cm x 71.1 cm)
*Panel*

**Judy Pelt**
*And There Was Light*
22" × 28" (55.9 cm × 71.1 cm)
*Production paper*

**Phyllis J. Friel**
*Ausonia*
24" × 30" (61 cm × 76.2 cm)
*007 Sanded paper*

**Anne Adams
Robertson Massie**

*Mykonos Harbor III*
28" x 36"  (71.1 cm x 91.4 cm)
*Fabriano Artistico 140 lb.
cold press*

**Marvin Yates**

*Stone's Antique Shop*
20" x 28"  (50.8 cm x 71.1 cm)
*Strathmore Hyplate*

**Stephen Quiller**
*Poppies, Sunflowers, and Sheep*
26" × 32" (66 cm × 81 cm)
*Crescent #5112 watercolor board*

**Stephen Quiller**
*The Twisted Spruce*
32" × 24" (81 cm × 61 cm)
*Crescent watercolor board*

**Christine Debrosky**
*Winter Wood*
19" x 25" (48.3 cm x 63.5 cm)
*Sanded pastel paper*

**Frank E. Zuccarelli**
*Pottersville*
18" x 24" (45.7 cm x 61 cm)
*Gesso- and pumice-treated
watercolor board*

**Coralie Alan Tweed**
*Bank of Poppies*
30" × 22" (76.2 cm × 55.9 cm)
*Pastel with gouache underpainting*
*Arches 130 lb. hot press watercolor*
*paper*

**Susan Ogilvie**
*Autumn Road*
17" × 13" (43.2 cm × 33 cm)
*La Carte pastel board*

**Stephen Quiller**
*March Light, San Juans*
23" × 35" (59 cm × 90 cm)
*Crescent watercolor board*

**Stephen Quiller**
*Beaver Pond, Deer Horn Park*
23" × 34" (58 cm × 86 cm)
*Crescent #5112 watercolor board*

**Gayle Fulwyler Smith**
*Canyon Overlook*
22" × 30" (55.9 cm × 76.2 cm)
E.H. Saunders 140 lb.
Media: Transparent watercolor, glazes, wet-on-wet painting

**Eric Wiegardt**
*University District*
21" × 29" (53.3 cm × 73.7 cm)
Arches 260 lb. cold press

**Jill Atkin**
*Field Burning III*
36" x 42" (91.4 cm x 106.7 cm)
*Ersta paper*

**Carole Chisholm Garvey**
*Indian Summer*
13.5" x 24" (34.3 cm x 60.3 cm)
*Canson paper*

**Helen H. Carmichael**
*Bass Head Lighthouse*
28" x 22"
(71.1 cm x 55.9 cm)
*Stretched canvas*

**Cory Staid**
*Verdant Landscape*
20" × 30"  (50.8 cm × 76.2 cm)
*Lin-Tex*

**Carolyn Lord**
*Bright and Breezy: Newport Beach*
22" × 15"  (55.9 cm × 38.1 cm)
*Arches 140 lb. cold press*

**Max R. Scharf**
*In the Beginning...Life*
30" x 40" (76 cm x 102 cm)
*Canvas*

**Max R. Scharf**
*The Gardens at Giverny*
30" x 40" (76 cm x 102 cm)
*Canvas*

**Anne Heywood**
*To the Ocean*
25" x 18" (63.5 cm x 45.7 cm)
*Granular board*

**Gregory Lysun**
*Morning-The Harbor*
32" × 42" (81.3 cm × 106.7 cm)
*Canvas*

**Roy Morrissey**
*One Horse Power*
12" × 16" (30.5 cm × 40.6 cm)
*Masonite*

**Pomm**

*Splendid Memories*
23" × 33"  (58.4 cm × 83.9 cm)
*Arches 140 lb. cold press*

**Max R. Scharf**
*Musee de Plein Air*
30" x 40" (76 cm x 102 cm)
*Canvas*

**Pamela G. Allnutt**
*The Coming of Winter*
30" × 40" (76.2 cm × 101.6 cm)
Pastel with goauche underpainting
Gesso- and marble dust-treated
100% rag cold press illustration board

**Pamela G. Allnutt**
*Early Thaw*
22" × 32" (55.9 cm × 81.3 cm)
Pastel with gouache underpainting
Gesso- and marble dust-prepared
100% rag cold press illustration board

**Milton Meyer**
*Boats of Honfleur*
24" × 31" (61 cm × 78.5 cm)
*Canson Mi-Teintes paper*

**Margot S. Schulzke**
*Salzburg Afternoon*
23" × 33" (58.4 cm × 83.8 cm)
*Sabretooth 2-ply rag board*

**75**

**Jean Warren**
*Preservation Park*
22" x 30"  (55.9 cm x 76.2 cm)
*Arches 140 lb. cold press*

**Yee Wah Jung**
*Country Side*
22" x 30"  (55.9 cm x 76.2 cm)
*Arches 140 lb.*
*Media:  Watercolor and acrylic mix*

**Nathalie J. Nordstrand, A.W.S.**
*Winter at Flat Ledge Quarry*
18.5" x 26"  (47 cm x 66 cm)
Fabriano Esportazione 300 lb.
*Media: Watercolor, gouache*

**Elsie K. Harris**
*Reawakening*
20" x 24" (51 cm x 61 cm)
*Linen*

**Elsie K. Harris**
*After Glow*
24" x 31" (61 cm x 79 cm)
*Linen*

**77**

**Anne Page**
*Mountain Goats
on the Edge*
36" x 28" (91.4 cm x 71.1 cm)
*Canvas*

**Jill Atkin**
*Afternoon Shallows*
36" x 42" (91.4 cm x 106.7 cm)
*Ersta paper*

**Bill Teitsworth**
*Lutz Farm*
10" x 11.5" (25 cm x 29 cm)
*Masonite board*

**Bill Teitsworth**
*Quarry*
18" x 11" (46 cm x 28 cm)
*Masonite board*

**Gloria Baker**
*The Reverance*
29" × 21" (73.7 cm × 53.3 cm)
*Arches 140 lb. cold press*

**George W. Kleopfer, Jr.**
*Osaka Castle and Friend*
23.75" × 29.25" (60.3 cm × 74.3 cm)
*2-ply illustration board*
*Media: Acrylic*

**Robert Eric Moore, N.A., A.W.S.**
*Snow and Wind Birds*
21" × 29" (53.3 cm × 73.7 cm)
*Arches 140 lb. cold press*

**Jill Atkin**
*Vantage Point II*
36" x 42" (91.4 cm x 106.7 cm)
*Ersta paper*

**Walter Brightwell**
*Return of the Hakers*
24" x 36" (61 cm x 91.4 cm)
*Panel*

**Emigdio Vasquez**
*Saturday Afternoon on Fourth Street*
24" × 30" (61 cm × 76.2 cm)
*Canvas*

**Gretchen H. Warren**
*Street Scene*
14" × 11" (35.6 cm × 27.9 cm)
*Canvas*

**Gerard F. Brommer**
*Mykonos Chapel*
11" x 15" (27.9 cm x 38.1 cm)
*Arches 300 lb. rough*
*Media: Watercolor, gouache, collage*

**Carlton B. Plummer**
*Vermont Mill*
21" x 28" (53.3 cm x 71.1 cm)
*Arches 140 lb. cold press*
*Transparent water-color, gouache*

**Bill Teitsworth**
*Heron Moon*
20" × 18" (51 cm × 46 cm)
*Masonite board*

**Jan Myers**
*Turquoise Trail in Autumn*
8" x 11" (20.3 cm x 27.9 cm)
*Stonehenge 180 lb. printmaking paper*

**Jan Myers**
*Evening Sagebrush*
11" x 15" (27.9 cm x 38.1 cm)
*Stonehenge 180 lb. printmaking paper*

**Gerald F. Brommer**
*Pemaquid*
36" x 48" (91 cm x 122 cm)
*Acrylic with washi (rice paper)*
*Canvas*

**Gerald F. Brommer**
*Greek Shadows*
36" x 48" (91 cm x 122 cm)
*Acrylic with washi (rice paper)*
*Canvas*

**Valentina Landin**
*Twin Trees*
7" x 5" (18 cm x 13 cm)
*Canvas*

**Lloyd Bakan**
*Spring*
24" x 30" (61 cm x 76 cm)
*Canvas*

**Anatoly Dverin**

*Monastery, Brugge Belgium*
17" × 22" (43.2 cm × 55.9 cm)
*Canson Ingres pastel paper, tint # 55*

**Violet Baxter**

*8th Floor View*
22.5" × 31" (57.2 cm × 78.1 cm)
*Canterbury handmade 170 lb. cover paper*

**Tim Flanagan**
*Autumn Interlude*
4" × 12" (10 cm × 30 cm)
*Masonite panel*

**Kathleen McDonough**
*Pond with Water Lilies*
44" × 52" (112 cm × 132 cm)
*Canvas*

**Donald L. Berry**
*Commuters*
28" × 50" (71.1 cm × 127 cm)
*Canvas*

**Emigdio Vasquez**
*The Orange Deli*
24" × 30" (61 cm × 76.2 cm)
*Canvas*

**Judith Futral Evans**
*Pond Sonata Triptych*
50" x 36" each (127 cm x 91 cm each)
*Canvas*

# Directory & Index

Martin R. Ahearn  44
102 Marmion Way
Rockport, MA 01966

Pamela G. Allnutt  74
1116 Wells Street
Iron Mountain, MI 49801

Jill Atkin  66, 79, 82
2092 Musket
Eugene, OR 97408

Steven L. Babecki  21
3774 Spinnaker Court
Fort Pierce, FL 34946

Lloyd Bakan  88
1721 Second Street, #103
Sacramento, CA 95814

Gloria Baker  81
2711 Knob Hill Drive
Evansville, IN 47711

Jeffrey L. Barnhart  7
568 Philadelphia Avenue
Chambersburg, PA 17201

Jann T. Bass  7
2700-B Walnut Street
Denver, CO 80205

Violet Baxter  36, 89
41 Union Street West, #402
New York, NY 10003-3208

Gaye Elise Beda  53
317 Second Avenue, #16
New York, NY 10003

Donald L. Berry  42, 91
P. O. Box 116, 331 West Main Street
Purcellville, VA 22131

Joan Boryta  20
133 East Main Street
Plainfield, MA 01070

Walter Brightwell  82
946 Reef Lane
Vero Beach, FL 32963

Gerald F. Brommer  15, 84, 87
11252 Valley Spring Lane
Studio City, CA 91602

Gerri Brutschy  49
94 Portola Avenue
Daly City, CA 94015

Richard Brzozowski  45
13 Fox Road
Plainville, CT 06062

Helen H. Carmichael  67
159 Jamaica Road
Tonawanda, NY 14150

Marge Chavooshian  25
222 Morningside Drive
Trenton, NJ 08618

Frank P. Corso  51, 55
44 Merrimac Street
Newburyport, MA 01980

Christine Debrosky  62
141 Mount View Road
Tillson, NY 12486

Harvey Dinnerstein  9
933 President Street
Brooklyn, NY. 11215

Kevin M. Donahue  19
2995 Hilltop Drive
Ann Arbor, MI 48103

Anatoly Dverin  23, 89
9 Oak Drive
Plainville, MA 02762

Judith Futral Evans  92, 93
34 Plaza Street, Apt 808
Brooklyn, NY 11238

Bonnie Fergus  22
67 Grandview Beach Road
Indian River, MI 49749

Tim Flanagan  90
Rural Route 1, Box 999
East Holden, ME 04429

Mark Flickinger  35
825 North 3rd
Arkansas City, KS 67005

Phyllis J. Friel  54, 59
920 Tenth Street
Hermosa Beach, CA 90254

Joyce Garner  26
7300 Happy Hollow Lane
Prospect, KY. 40059

Carole Chisholm Garvey  46, 48, 66
68 Chine Way
Osterville, MA 02655

Barbara Goodspeed  27
11 Holiday Point Road
Sherman, CT 06784

Becky Haletky  40
128 Liberty Street
Rockland, MA 02370

Elsie K. Harris  77
1043 Heather Hills Lane
Lexington, KY. 40511

Anne Heywood  36, 70
85 Ashley Drive
East Bridgewater, MA 02333

Howard Huizing  52
145 S. Olive Street
Orange, CA 92666

Sandra Humphries  3 8
3503 Berkeley Place NE
Albuquerque, NM 87106

Philip Jamison  17
104 Price Street
West Chester, PA 19382

Joe Jaqua  25
300 Stony Point Road
Santa Rosa, CA 95401

Bruce G. Johnson  37
953 E. 173rd Street
South Holland, IL 60473-3529

Jack Jones  8
391 Maple Street
Danvers, MA 01923

Yee Wah Jung  76
5468 Bloch Street
San Diego, CA 92122

Linda Kessler  22
54 Orange Street, #4-H
Brooklyn, NY 11201

Dong Kingman  47
21 W. 58th Street
New York, NY 10019

Everett Raymond Kinstler  37
15 Gramercy Park S.
New York, NY 10003

George W. Kleopfer, Jr.  81
2110 Briarwood Boulevard
Arlington, TX 76013

Kristi Krafft  39
4782 Encinal Cyn. Road
Malibu, CA 90265

Connie Kuhnle  14
10215 Young Avenue
Rockford, MI 49341

Valentina Landin  88
P. O. Box 72
Palm Desert, CA 92261

Christopher Leeper  16
4263 Lake Road
Youngstown, OH 44511

Monroe Leung  29
1990 Abajo Drive
Monterey Park, CA. 91754

Donna Levinstone  30
1601 3rd Avenue, 17F
New York, NY 10128

Petr Liska  13
13410 Keating Court
Rockville, MD 20853

Lynne Lockhart  48
302 Bay Street
Berlin, MD 21811

Carol Lopatin  24, 28
105 North Union Street
Alexandria, VA 22314

Carolyn Lord  68
1993 De Vaca Way
Livermore, CA 94550-5609

Gregory Lysun  71
481 Winding Road North
Ardsley, NY 10502-2701

Fred MacNeill  11
23 Dana Road
Concord, MA 01742

Ward P. Mann  58
77 Rocky Neck Avenue
Gloucester, MA 01930

Margaret M. Martin  44
69 Elmwood Avenue
Buffalo, NY 14201

Babette Martino  43
1435 Manor Lane
Blue Bell, PA 19422

Anne Adams Robertson Massie  60
3204 Rivermont Avenue
Lynchburg, VA 24503

Giovanni Martino  31
1435 Manor Lane
Blue Bell, PA 19422

Benjamin Mau  52
1 LaTeer Drive
Normal, IL 61761

Kathleen McDonough  90
338 Maple Street
Carlisle, MA 01741

Fred L. Messersmith  12
726 N. Boston Avenue
DeLand, FL 32724

Milton Meyer  75
5487 East Oxford Avenue
Englewood, CO. 80111

Clark G. Mitchell  18
100 Firethorn Drive
Rohnert Park, CA 94928-1332

Robert Eric Moore  81
111 Cider Hill Road
York, ME 03909-5213

Glenn Moreton  49. 50, 53
9200 Edwards Way, 1011
Adelphi, MD 20783

Roy Morrisey  71
1837 East Campus Way
Hemet, CA 92544

Elizabeth M. Mowry  32
287 Marcott Road
Kingston, NY 12401

Murray Muldofsky  39
1216 Ocean Parkway
Brooklyn, NY 11215

Jan Myers  86
8309 Benton Way
Arvada, CO 80003

Joyce Nagel  6
6 Honey Locust Circle
Hilton Head Island, SC 29926

Nathalie J. Nordstrand  76
384 Franklin Street
Reading, MA 01867

Susan Ogilvie  63
P.O. Box 59
Pt. Hadlock, WA 98339

Desmond O'Hagan  33
2882 South Adams Street
Denver, CO 80210

Cheryl O'Halloran-McLeod  56
1318 Belleview Avenue
Plainfield, NJ 07060

Don O'Neill  8
3723 Tibbetts Street
Riverside, CA 92506

Anne Page  78
P. O. Box 159
Saratoga, NY 82331

Gloria Paterson  38
9090 Barnstaple Lane
Jacksonville, FL 32257

Judy Pelt  14, 59
2204 Ridgmar Plaza, #2
Fort Worth, TX 76116

Barry G. Pitts  54
P. O. Box 14526
Long Beach, CA 90803

Carlton B. Plummer  84
10 Monument Hill Road
Chelmsford, MA 01824

Pomm  72
4865 Hartwick Street
Los Angeles, CA 90041

Stephen Quiller  61, 64
P. O. Box 160 120 Creede Avenue
Creede, CO 81130

Diana Randolph  18
Rural Route 1, Box 66-C
Drummond, WI 54832

Judith S. Rein  47
10064 W Greenlawn Drive
La Porte, IN 46350

Dorothy Sandlin  6
3239 West 205th Street
Olympia Fields, IL 60461

Max R. Scharf  69, 73
1416 Willowbrook Cove
St. Louis, MO 63146

Margot S. Schulzke  75
1840 Little Creek Road
Auburn, CA 95602

Kathy Shumway-Tunney  19
105 Walnut Street
Bordentown, NJ 08505

Gayle Fulwyler Smith  65
P.O. Box 56
Embudo, NM 87531

Cory Staid  68
P.O. Box 592A
Kennebunkport, ME 04046

Paul Strisik  20
123 Marmion Way
Rockport, MA 01966

Judith Surowiec  34, 41
2795 Ashton Tree Court
Dacula, GA 30211

Merriel Taylor  56
22800 Latrake Road
Plymouth, CA 95669

Bill Teitsworth  80, 85
Rural Route 6, Box 6427
Moscow, PA 18444

Lois Salmon Toole  40
561 North Street
Chagrin Falls, OH 44022

Lynn Tornberg  13, 57
19 Mill Street
Manchester, MA 01944

Lorrie B. Turner  29, 46
14 Village Drive
Huntington, NY 11743

Coralie Alan Tweed  31, 32, 42 63
915 East 8th Avenue
Johnson City, TN 37601

Susan Lucas Updyke  34
10 Brentwood
Bristol, TN 37620

Emigdio Vasquez  83, 91
555 North Cypress Street
Orange, CA 92667

Lawrence Wallin  10
895 Toro Canyon Road
Santa Barbara, CA 93108

Gretchen H. Warren  83
1895 Bluff Street Apt. C
Boulder, CO 80304

Jean Warren  76
22541 Old Santa Cruz Highway
Los Gatos, CA 95030

William Welch  12
P. O. Box 2847
Nantucket, MA 02584

Murray Wentworth  52
132 Central Street
Norwell, MA 02061

Wilma Wethington  7
2 Linden Drive
Wichita, KS 67206

Eric Wiegardt  65
Box 1114
Ocean Park, WA 98640

Marvin Yates  60
1457 Highway 304
Hernando, MS 38632

Frank E. Zuccarelli  62
61 Appleman Road
Somerset, NJ 08873